Ho...
Disci...
Without Damage

Judy Helm Wright aka "Auntie Artichoke"

Finding the Heart of the Story in the Journey of Life

Part of the "77 Ways to Parent" Series

How to Discipline Without Damage

Judy Helm Wright aka Auntie Artichoke

Artichoke Press
2400 West Central, Missoula MT 59801
Web site: www.ArtichokePress.com
Parenting Blog: www.AskAuntieArtichoke.com
For additional parenting, wellness, life-story writing, end-of-life books and programs please see our website or contact us directly.

All rights reserved. No part of this publication may be reproduced, stored in a retrieval system, or transmitted in any form or by any means without prior written permission from the publisher.

Self-published in the United States of America by:

ARTICHOKE PRESS LLC

Medical Disclaimer: Please use this book as a guide and suggestions, not as medical or psychological advice. Judy H. Wright is not a doctor, licensed counselor or professional consultant, she is a parent educator and family advocate. If you are concerned about some aspect of your child's development, or your own mental health, do not hesitate to seek professional help.

Affiliate Disclaimer: Some of the resources and programs that are recommended in this eBook pay a small commission to the author when you buy them. This commission is used to further the goals of those who protect children, so we appreciate your support. You pay the same amount, but the company pays Artichoke Press for the referral.

Dedicated with love

to my children and grandchildren

who have taught me so much in life

Hello and thank you for wanting to know more about positive discipline.

My name is Judy and I live in the beautiful state of Montana. I am a parent educator who loves working with people who live and interact with children on a daily basis, just like you. It is such a pleasure to expand my notes, observations and research into eBooks and tele-classes.

My husband, Dwain, and I have six adult children and ten grandchildren. We consider assisting them to be independent and loving people our greatest accomplishment and hardest job. We didn't always do the "right things." I yelled too much and he ignored too much, but we kept starting over. And over. And over. And we read, studied and tried new techniques and ideas for gaining a happier home and family. We also watched and learned from families in my parenting classes and other classes that we attended as a couple.

Successful Families Look For Solutions

Most parents are doing a great job. Most families I meet are willing to look for tips and techniques to enhance good relationships. We all need reinforcement and some new ideas to stay on track. Sometimes we need the words to say or examples of how other families handled similar situations. Most importantly, we need encouragement and empowerment.

There are so many valuable resources out there for struggling parents, but we need to be teachable and ask for help when we need it. The easiest thing to do is give up and let the TV raise your children while hoping for the best. The higher road that each of you have chosen is to make your family your top priority in life today and every day.

Be a Present Parent

Congratulations! Remember you don't have to be a perfect parent, but you need to be a present parent. They need your presence and attention much more than presents from Toys-R-Us. Remember that 90% of success is just showing up every day and caring.

One hundred years from now, it will not matter what kind of car you drove, what you did for a living, how many hours you stayed at the office to finish a report, how clean your house was or how many "things" you had acquired. What will matter is that you affected eternity and changed the world because you took the time and effort to be important in the life of your child.

Good luck and God bless. You do an important work.

Judy Helm Wright

Table of Contents

Discipline without Damage
- Respect and Kindness
- Model Acceptable Behavior
- Alternatives to Abuse

Discipline, but never punish
- Outward or Inner Directed?
- Time Out for Children—Does it Work?
- So, Is Time Out An Effective Discipline
- Time Out For Adults
- Focus on solutions, not excuses
- Step back to see a new perspective
- Take an Adult Time Out To Regroup

CHAPTER BREAK ???
- Hand Over Heart Quick Meditation (great info but needs to be somewhere more effective)
- Peace for Parents
- Use "I Statements"

Natural and Logical Consequences
- Natural Consequences
- Logical Consequences
- It's okay to Make Mistakes
- Failure Is Part of Success
- Let Noticeable Consequences Take Their Natural Course

Catch them doing things right.
- Discouragement is the basis for most failure and lack of even trying to take risks.

Teach without anger, shame or blame
- Shaming and blaming never result in behavior changes, but in resentment and bruised souls.
- There is no such thing as a "good" or "bad" child.
- Create consistent boundaries

Separate the deed from the doer
- Non-Verbal Reminders
- Use encouragement instead of criticism
- Say Yes instead of No
- Guidelines for What You Can Do
- Tell Them What You Do Want
- Add some information here

Spanking and screaming are not affective teachers.
When You Scream, You Can't Hear
Eliminate "who's at fault."
Be aware of your facial expressions.
Treat each child as an individual.
Be careful of using abusive adjectives—they really hurt.
Recognize effort and improvement:
)(This whole section may be moved somewhere else, It just takes up room here. Or then again, it may further explain what I am trying to teach)
Don't punish them for telling the truth.
Praise in public, correct in private
Distinguish between minor mishaps and major problems.
Model Forgiveness
Be curious not furious. Ask questions.
(blah blah,,,,I need to redo this part.)

A final note to parents
About The Author
Resources for Parents, Teachers and other Caring Adults

Note to me; add affiliate links, links to other books in the 77 Ways to Parent Series, Update the resource page. Put the text box at least 100 pixels so it will go side to side. Break the paragraphs into 2-3 sentences. Do we want to add photos? If so they must go clear across the page, maybe just three or four per book. Not overwhelming.

Discipline without Damage

Our job as parents, coaches, mentors and extended family is to raise socially responsible adults who can be independent and contributing members of society. To do this, we must teach them the difference between right and wrong, assist them in understanding all decisions carry consequences and to be self-disciplined.

Our overall goal is to communicate to the child, "You are okay and we love you unconditionally, but the behavior in this instance needs to be corrected."

We want to be available to provide support and guidance by maintaining respect and enhancing the self-esteem and confidence of the child.

We all make mistakes, errors and dumb choices. In order for our children to learn from the experience and move on, it is important to impress upon them how we handle our own mistakes.

Are we intent on punishment, retaliation and force or are we more concerned with teaching a life lesson that will hopefully correct the behavior and not harm the spirit of the child?

Respect and Kindness

Discipline is not necessarily something we "do to" our children, but rather a system for helping them to lead responsible, productive lives. Sometimes that includes corrective measures when an action or behavior was not in the best interest and safety of the child or those around them, and sometimes it includes preventative discipline.

The preventative discipline includes allowing your child to be a problem solver, to "own" a problem and come up with a win-win solution.

It also means that providing a situation isn't harmful, the child is allowed to suffer the natural or logical consequences of their choices.

Experience really is the best teacher and many parents jump in to soon to "save" the child, which actually sends a subtle message that we don't think they can handle life's problems. They can and will, when you act as an advisor and supporter, rather than a boss or ultimate authority.

Model Acceptable Behavior

If your parenting methods include abuse of any kind; physical, sexual, emotional or verbal, please get help to stop as soon as possible.

You owe it to your children and yourself to break the bonds and cycle of abuse and get help. Adults are supposed to safeguard and protect the young among us, but you may be reacting without conscious thought.

Perhaps you are repeating patterns learned in your family of origin or not know any other methods of parenting. People who abuse children are not necessarily crazy or evil. They are usually people who don't feel very good about themselves, are angry at the world and have not learned more positive ways to handle frustration.

Alternatives to Abuse

In this section, you will find a number of different approaches to discipline that won't damage the spirit of your precious children. Unfortunately, none will work if you haven't acknowledged that what you were doing in the past was harmful and that your family deserves a more nurturing environment. I am not a psychologist or a counselor, but I know there are good ones out there who can assist you in shifting your paradigm of discipline to a more loving and respectful relationship.

Change is possible. I see it every day in families I work with, including my own. You are a good, kind and loving person or you wouldn't be reading this book and attending these classes, so I encourage you to take the steps that will change the lives of your children and their children.

You can do it. I believe in you.

Discipline, but never punish

Discipline comes from the root word Disciple and means, "training to act in accordance with rules, instruction or learning, a regimen that develops or improves skills." This puts parents, teachers, coaches and other adults who are in a position of authority in the position of a leader and teacher who wants to train and encourage.

Discipline is accomplished when a child is shown how to behave in a more acceptable way. It does not have to be physical or done in anger.

To punish someone is to treat them harshly and to inflict a penalty for some offense or fault, and it becomes child abuse when the adult is deliberately injuring a child in physical, verbal or sexual ways. **One never learns from punishment, except to punish others**.

A friend's 4-year-old child once said after receiving a spanking for an infraction, "I can't wait till I'm big enough to hit someone." Needless to say, that was the last time they used corporal punishment.

Outward or Inner Directed?

Parental discipline is a learning process, which helps us to both correct and prevent problems. When we use reward and punishment to teach self-control we set up power struggles and situations that encourages rebellion, resistance and arguments.

That style creates an outward directed action, whereas if we want to develop inner self-control and confidence, we must include them in the teaching process.

When we give our children choices within appropriate limits and help them be aware of natural and logical consequences of those choices, we help them gain some control over various areas of their lives.

Chocies---needs more clarification. Maybe move something else here.

Time Out for Children—Does it Work?

I am not completely convinced that time outs work for children. It seems to me that the consequences need to be tied some way to the mistake in order for the discipline to become effective. However, I am convinced that parents need to step back at times and reflect on the fact that they are teachers who are training the next generation, instead of giving in to the impulse to scream, smack or threaten.

"Get down from the table top right now! What are you doing? Floors are for standing on, tables are for eating. You need a time out, young lady. You go to your room and think about how you have been acting today."

So little Mary, 4, goes to her room with a sulky look on her face, but is quickly lost in a game with her dolls and toys. When her mother comes to tell her that she can come out, she is so engrossed in playing that she barely looks up, completely forgetting why she was sent to time out in the first place.

So, Is Time Out An Effective Discipline

Yes, but only when it is age appropriate (one minute for each year of age) and then followed by a discussion at eye level of why the action was unacceptable. There has to be some conversation or connection to the actual event or misbehavior for it to be used as a teaching tool. It has been my experience that the consequences need to be tied in some tangible way to the mistake in order for the discipline to become long lasting. Perhaps a more effective teaching discipline would be to have Mary scrub the table and chairs.

When the room is in chaos, the kids are fighting, the phone is ringing, the potatoes are burning and the baby is crying all at the same time, the natural reaction is to explode. Even the act of seeing the bike in the driveway, again, is enough to make the blood boil and the steam come out of our ears.

Time Out For Adults

I am convinced that parents need to step back at times and reflect on the fact that they are teachers and training the next generation, instead of giving in to the impulse to scream, smack or threaten.

In 15 minutes (often you don't get the luxury of one minute for each year of age, but wouldn't it be nice?) you will have calmed down some and the child will be ready to offer solutions.

Focus on solutions, not excuses

Do not allow him to offer excuses, only solutions. Allowing him to own the problem and the consequences makes it a much more effective learning experience for both of you. Taking time out before a discussion gives both the parent and the child time to regain some perspective and come up with a much more meaningful solution than one handed out in a moment of anger.

An example from one mother

Sandy, Mother of 3 shared with a parenting class some excellent advice on dealing with children;

> "Many times when the kids seemed to have 'an attitude' that I knew could rapidly lead to a confrontation, I made them go in the kitchen and have a peanut butter sandwich or some cheese and crackers and then meet me in 20 minutes to discuss things. Frequently, they were simply hungry or thirsty and needed to get some protein and carbohydrates in their body to regulate the blood sugar. It is amazing how many arguments were forestalled by a full belly. Finding out that active 11-13 year old boys needed 3,000 calories a day to operate and grow, explained why they were cranky a lot!"

Step back to see a new perspective

It is better by far for you to give the child some warning and say " I am so angry right now that I am afraid I will say or do something that would make both of us sorry, so I am going to go in the bedroom and calm down for a few minutes. Meet me in the living room in 15 minutes and we will discuss it. But, in the meantime, I strongly suggest you not bother me and that you spend the time thinking about solutions to the problem."

You want to have the misbehavior stop, but not damage my child's spirit" "That was a rotten thing for her to have done, but she is not a rotten child" "She is a good child who made a bad choice" "Is this worth ruining the evening over?" "This too (or two, in the case of toddlers) shall pass."

Relax somewhat by taking a deep breath to the count of four, hold for the count of four and release to the count of four, while you are thinking or saying aloud "Be calm". Now, do it again at least three times. You can feel your muscles unwind and your head clear somewhat. You will feel more in command of your voice and your actions.

Take an Adult Time Out To Regroup

You have my permission to take a time out whenever you need it.

Children need firm and kind discipline and we can't offer that when we are angry or out of control ourselves. A few minutes of reflection, prayer or deep breathing can give us a new prospective on life and the crayon drawings on the living room wall.

You do the most important work in the world and twenty years from now, it will be a funny family story about Mary on the dining room table. In reflection you will both realize that tables can be washed or even replaced, but close relationships and respectful guidance are priceless.

CHAPTER BREAK ???

Hand Over Heart Quick Meditation (great info but needs to be somewhere more effective)

This technique was taught to me by a brilliant little boy (see my article on Indigo Kids-Born to lead, Hard to Manage at http://www.articlesbyjudy.com).

Simply put your primary hand over your heart and say, "I am safe." Breath in and out while repeating the mantra. This little boy was living in a difficult situation and found a way to self-sooth and ground himself, because the adults in his environment could not.

This is powerful meditation that you can do anywhere, anytime and no one even has to know you are calming yourself down. Teach it to your children so they have an alternative to anger in frustrating times.

You, too, may have an Indigo or Star child who is destined to do great things in life and is not easily directed by usual methods. There is another parenting book on its way to you about these children. Keep your eyes peeled.

Peace for Parents

When the room is in chaos, the kids are fighting, the phone is ringing, the potatoes are burning and the baby is crying at the same time, the natural reaction is to explode. Even the act of seeing the bike in the driveway, again, is enough to make the blood boil and the steam come out of our ears.

It is better by far for you to give the child some warning and say, " I am so angry right now that I am afraid I will say or do something that would make both of us sorry, so I am going to go in the bedroom and calm down for a few minutes. Meet me in the living room in 15 minutes and we will discuss it. But, in the meantime, I strongly suggest you not bother me and that you spend the time thinking about solutions to the problem."

In 15 minutes you will have calmed down some and the child will be ready to offer solutions. Do not allow him to offer excuses, only solutions. Allowing him to own the problem and the consequences makes it a much more effective learning experience for both of you. Taking time out before a discussion allows both the parent and the child to regain some perspective and come up with a much more meaningful solution than one handed out in a moment of anger.

Sandy, Mother of Three
Many times when the kids seemed to have "an attitude" that I knew could rapidly lead to a confrontation, I made them go in the

kitchen and have a peanut butter sandwich or some cheese and crackers and then meet me in 20 minutes to discuss things. Frequently, they were simply hungry or thirsty and needed to get some protein and carbs in their body to regulate the blood sugar. It is amazing how many arguments were forestalled by a full belly. Finding out that an active 11-13 year old boy needed 3,000 calories a day to operate and grow, explained why they were cranky a lot!

Use "I Statements"

Whenever we start a dialog with a child with the word "you" defenses go up and they anticipate being scolded or told to do something they probably won't want to do.

For example:

- You stop that this minute
- You didn't do that right
- You are acting like a baby
- You know better than to kick me

However, when parents begin the sentence with an "I," there is no accusation or blame attached and it doesn't feel like it is directed at them directly.

"I" statements are actually just statements of how you feel and no one can argue with your feelings. When a child's behavior is unacceptable to a parent because in some way it is interfering with our enjoyment or our rights, we own the problem. By using" I' messages, we are sharing our perceptions, not making judgments about the child.

For example:

- I don't like to step over toys on the floor. It makes me feel like I could slip and fall on them. Please keep them in one place or we will have to put them away for the rest of the day.
- I am concerned because…
- This is the way I see it…
- I worry when…

The best "I" message of all is "I love you."

Natural and Logical Consequences

The only way any system of discipline will work is if your child knows that you will always follow through. You must set boundaries as a family and be consistent in either allowing natural consequences to take place or imposing logical ones that will encourage learning the lesson.

Natural Consequences

Natural consequences are what happen naturally when a choice is made or not made. If you choose to not pay the electric bill, eventually the electricity will be turned off. If your child doesn't show up for baseball practice, he will be dropped from the team.

Logical Consequences

If there is no natural consequence, then the next best teacher is a logical consequence- one that is relevant to the error in judgment, so that a connection is made in the mind and conscience of the child. For instance: If they break another's child's toy, they have to replace it. If they are rude and demanding, after a warning to stop the unacceptable behavior, they may have to miss the birthday party..

It's okay to Make Mistakes

The most important teaching moments you will have will be when they finally "get it." For many children, that means a number of tries or bouncing against the boundaries and standards of the family.

We need to help prepare them for the real world by eliminating incorrect or harmful behavior as soon as it appears. We want to teach the life skills and attitudes necessary to be successful in every aspect of life.

It isn't always easy or convenient to enforce consequences, but doing so will shorten the learning curve. Once the child knows that you mean what you say and will follow through, they will have more respect for you and ultimately for themselves.

With work (and it does involve more time and energy on your part) you can teach your child to develop a sense of responsibility. Your assistance will enable them to think before acting, as well as come to an understanding that appropriate behavior leads to pleasant consequences and inappropriate behavior leads to discomfort and inconvenience.

Failure Is Part of Success

I have found that people who have overcome adversity, failure or disappointment have become more resilient in all areas of life. In researching for my latest book *Out of Balance? Be a Bounce Back Person,* available at www.artichokepress.com there is strong evidence that overcoming failure and mistakes actually makes you a better problem-solver in life.

The best way for any of us to learn is by experiencing the consequences of our choices. Children need to be taught that there are consequences for their actions-good and bad. Sometimes parents and loved ones actually teach negative habits by default.

For example:

If your child knows that your family values responsibility, he will remember to get his school papers ready the night before, or he will have to do without them the next day. However, if you drop what you are doing and bring them to him at school, he learns to manipulate the system and that there really are no bad consequences for his forgetfulness.

Parents too often rescue their children from negative consequences. Yet, if we want to have self-disciplined children who practice responsibility and engage in appropriate conduct, we occasionally need to allow them to feel the pain of their choices. When we follow through with consequences, it makes life easier for everyone in the family, schoolroom and world of work because we aren't going through the same problems again and again.

Let Noticeable Consequences Take Their Natural Course

As our children grew into adolescence, we always volunteered to drive the car pool. We knew that even if our kids didn't want to be as close to us as we would have liked them to be, at least we could be within a few feet of each other in a car. The kids eventually grew to love us driving because we would often treat them to ice cream. Some of the best parenting advice we ever got was listening in on the conversations in the back of the mini-van.

One time I remember in particular was a group of high school girls on the soccer team discussing what their parents did when the girls stayed out past curfew or drank. The unanimous consensus was that most parents choose grounding as a punishment, and that it was not a deterrent to future actions.

The girls admitted that they sometimes decided to stay later at a party because they knew the only consequence was a bawling out and not being allowed to go out for a week. They also knew they could talk their way out of the grounding in 3-5 days. They laughed and said that by five days most parents and kids couldn't remember what the grounding was for! When I asked them (much to my daughter's embarrassment) what would have been effective, they said having to do some sort of work, or write an essay or something that would have forced them to think a little harder about their choices.

You will need to be wise enough to let choices, especially those with noticeable consequences to take their natural course. However, it is important to note that if the goal is to teach a lesson, you must be willing to discuss what just happened while it is still fresh in your child's mind. They need to be taught, because they do not know instinctively, that bad decisions always catch up with us and good decisions make us, and those around us, happy.

Michael, age 16

In my family, if you screw up, you really have to work to earn the trust back. My dad grew up on a farm and he thinks we have it too easy and so when we get in trouble, we have to do physical labor as a reminder. Sometimes it is to scrub the bathrooms, paint the garage or mow the lawn for the neighbors all summer or something really hard so that we remember and don't do it again. My friends think it is really harsh, but boy I think twice before I do dumb things. One time my brother and I kept arguing and fighting and so my parents made us build a storage shed together. We were really mad at the time, but now we have this neat shed and we learned to cooperate.

Catch them doing things right.

For everything a child does wrong, he does 19 things right. Children who only receive attention when they misbehave or make poor judgments soon learn to blame others and avoid responsibility. For more information on this problem see my special report, "It's Not My Fault" at www.artichokepress.com. If you have a hard time saying positive phrases, try this idea:

Find a time when you are really happy to be her parent and tell her using the "I feel" method. "I feel so proud of you when I see how kind you are to Grandma." "I feel so happy when I see you and your brother playing well together."

Studies show that it takes 13 positive statements to counteract the effect of a negative statement. If you make a point of expressing positive feeling at least twice as often as you do negative ones, you will be on the road to good family communication and a more confident child.

Go to www.ArtichokePress.com and request the free report on 15 encouraging phrases and try to incorporate them into your daily communication with your kids. You will be amazed at how much more cooperative they become when they realize you do see their good side and not just notice every time they screw up.

Discouragement is the basis for most failure and lack of even trying to take risks.

I divide the words when working with parents into "dis"couragement and "en"couragement. To "dis" someone is to put them down to take away from their status or accomplishments. When we discourage our children we take away their courage to take risks. They begin tie a failure of any kind with a loss of love from you, their most important advocate. They would rather not try at all than risk your disapproval. However, on the flip side, to encourage is to give them the right to make mistakes, to effectively say, "Hey, it's okay if you take a risk and fail. My love is unconditional and is not tied to what you do or accomplish."

Ellie, age 16

Once, when my mom first started work, I wanted to surprise her with dinner when she got home, only I didn't know how to cook. I was only 12 and she had always done everything for the whole family. She walked in and the kitchen was a mess! I thought for sure she would start yelling but she just said, "Oh well, you will get better with more practice." I am a pretty good cook now, even though my favorite is still mac-n-cheez.

Teach without anger, shame or blame

Shaming and blaming never result in behavior changes, but in resentment and bruised souls.

All parents get angry sometimes. Even caring ones or your children's friend's parents who do everything right, according to your child. However, when we are angry, old patterns come rolling to the surface and we react in ways that we ordinarily would not. When we lose complete control we say and do things to our children that we would be hesitant to do to an enemy. We yell, threaten, insult and storm around the house.

Not only do hurtful words strike the heart of the child, but also the *inference* of what he thinks you meant. So when a glass of milk is spilled and the parent yells, "How could you be so clumsy? Milk costs a lot of money and now I have to drop what I'm doing and run to the store to have enough milk for breakfast." The child not only hears the words, but feels:

- He is a clumsy person
- He is costing the family money they don't have
- It is all his fault that his mother is tired and has to run to the store
- Because of his actions, the whole family is suffering

When in reality, a 20-cent glass of milk was spilled. The family would need more milk soon anyway. The family lost 20 cents in milk, but the child lost a great deal of confidence. How much better it would have been for the Mother to say, "I see the milk is spilled. Here is a sponge." When things are going wrong it is not the right time to try to correct personality flaws or make the child feel worse than he already does. Just deal with the event, not the person.

And if we do blow it and get mad and lose our temper, then apologize. Explain that life is a progression of learning and relearning lessons. We have the right to get angry; we simply don't have the right to attack the child's personality or character. Parents send daily messages relating to how competent and worthwhile their children are. The development of confidence and self-esteem is a cumulative process that happens a little bit every day. If in general, a child is nurtured positively, a bad experience or two will not have a major impact on their view of self. However, if a child has been put down every day, even a series of great experiences will not be enough to fill that emptiness, or love bank as one young girl told me, inside them.

> *Savannah, 4 years old*
> *My mom told me that inside our heart, we each have a love bank, kinda like a piggy bank. When people say good things about you, or you feel happy, or you do nice things for other people, it is like you put pennies in the bank. When someone yells at you or hits you, it is like they are taking the pennies. So you have to find more pennies to put in your love bank. Talking to you feels like I am putting pennies in, 'cause I feel happy inside. Do you?*

If you came from a background of parental blaming and shaming, you may not be aware of how often you are falling into the very patterns that you hated as a child. Children tend to feel responsible for family trouble, especially when the parents are having a lot of marital discord or are divorcing. Many adults who were children from divorced homes say that the worst part of the whole thing was the overwhelming blame they felt. In retrospect they wished their parents had been more open with them and cooperative with the other spouse. To hear a parent bad-mouth and belittle the absent parent and then tell the child "You are just like your mother/father" was heart breaking.

The key thing to remember about shame and guilt is that the action may have been a mistake, but the child never is.

There is no such thing as a "good" or "bad" child.

Convey with every act and word that your love is constant. Tell them you love them every day. Make sure they understand that your love and affection is not dependent upon them being "a good child." It is too much responsibility for anyone, child or adult, to be "good" all the time.

It is never so black and white. Most of us live in perpetual shades of gray where we struggle to be a little better today than we were yesterday and hope that tomorrow we will remember what we have learned and try to incorporate it into our daily lives. We are all on a pathway of learning and as such we all screw up occasionally or slip back into old habits.

Josh, 8 years old:
"One time I wet my pants at school because the teacher would not let me go to the bathroom. She said I should have gone when it was lunchtime. I just felt awful and the nurse called my mom at work to come and get me. I was so afraid she would yell at me or be mad but she

just held out her arms and gave me a hug.
I really needed that hug.

Create consistent boundaries

Children, whether they are 2 or 12, feel more confident when they know that you are in charge and that their environment is predictable and safe. Consistency means always following through with what you say and acting the same each time the same behavior occurs. Your child will be able to predict that every time he gets in the car, the key will not turn the engine on until all the seat belts are buckled.

We all need to know the boundaries of what is expected of us. Can you imagine entering a marathon and not being given the rules, map or directions? You could probably follow the crowd, but how would you know they were headed in the right direction? Each family should develop a few family rules and instill boundaries in daily life. For instance, in our family, calling each other disrespectful names was not tolerated. If a child was rude or disrespectful to a parent, they would soon know they had crossed the line. If they chose to speak disrespectfully, they automatically chose to forgo TV and electronic games for the evening.

Consistency is the number one factor in successful families: consistency in love, respect, cooperation and expectations. However, it is important to point out that consistent is not the same as rigid. Consistent boundaries are pretty predictable. A child can count on dinner being at six o'clock or there about. They need to know that bedtime is 8:30 on school nights and that homework is done before playtime. But, sometimes in life, opportunities arise that make boundaries and rules flexible. A relative visits from out of town; it might be okay for the kids to stay up until 9:30 one night to enjoy the experience. As long as the family knows that in general, there is a structure they can count on and limits to what is accepted and what is not, they will flourish in a system that gives them guidelines and direction.

Serra, 16 years old

In our family there was a very delicate line on what was expected and what was tolerated. We could tell by the look on my Dad's face when we had stepped over the line. Not that he ever "punished or hit" us. It was more that we didn't want to disappoint him because he loved us so much.

Separate the deed from the doer

When Joey takes money from the top of your dresser, he doesn't automatically become a thief. He is still Joey, the son you love, who has made a bad choice. We can and should be angry at the choice and behavior.

It is imperative that Joey understands it is wrong to take anything without permission and amends must be made to correct the problem. Use natural or logical consequences to teach, but don't damage his spirit. A natural consequence would be to return the money and then do extra chores to show remorse.

Inappropriate behavior can be thought of as an opportunity for teaching your child about choices and how they affect everyone around us. Another way of looking at misbehavior is that the child is telling us they need our help in directing their behavior. As parents, we need to notice when we are given signals.

To ignore negative behavior is to send a message that you will tolerate that kind of action. Negative actions will increase if you ignore them or treat them as no big deal. **Positive behavior will increase if we give it attention.**

Remember, your job is to teach. How will your child ever know or recognize right from wrong if you don't teach him the difference?

If you have ever been embarrassed by a toddler who threw a tantrum in the supermarket, you know how frustrated you and the child felt. The easiest path would be to get angry and yell at the child or hand him a candy bar to shut him up. But remember you are a teacher.

One of the ways I found effective to short circuit a meltdown for an excitable child was to hold her very tightly and talk softly in her ear. I would whisper that I knew how upset she was and that I was going to help her calm down. I would continue talking softly and list all the people who loved her.

Her body would gradually relax. When she was calm, I congratulated her on learning new ways to be in control of her emotions.

As she aged, this daughter told me that when she is over stimulated at work, she whispers to herself to regain the calmness she needs to do her work.

If you have a baby who is colicky, swaddling (wrapping tightly in a blanket and tucking in the edges) works wonders. It is a secure feeling.

Some children take longer to learn a lesson or appear to repeat the same mistake over and over. But different children have different needs. Remember the ultimate lesson you are trying to teach is for the child to self-discipline. Be very careful you do not confuse the child with the behavior. They are two separate and distinct things.

Issue a warning, but mean it.

Warnings seem to be the most effective among young children who have trouble remembering. So when you give a brief reminder of the appropriate or inappropriate behavior and the consequences,

You can usually get a proper response without going to an elaborate and time consuming discipline like time out. For instance, "Jennifer, you know that you may play with play-doh only on the table. Clean it up and play with it correctly or it will have to be put away for the rest of the day." Or even better, "play-doh, table (pointing), now."

Such a brief specific warning may be all you need, but you must be willing to carry through with the consequences as promised. Speak in a 'matter of fact' tone of voice about the limits and rules and the outcome of continued misbehavior. Too often we threaten in anger, exaggerate grossly and then fail to follow through.

It may be inconvenient for you to follow through, because you may want to stay at the beach or you may not want to shut off the TV, but if you have issued a warning, then mean what you say. It is your prompt compliance with the terms of the warning that will quickly convince your child you mean business.

Non-Verbal Reminders

One family we knew had code words for each child to remind them when they needed to calm down. So when Jack's mom held her hand to her ear and said, "Is that a train I hear in the distance?" Jack knew he had been reminded about his behavior without being scolded or embarrassed in front of friends.

A method we used to monitor actions in a public place was to raise one finger, then two fingers. The kids knew that if we raised the third finger, they would be removed from the activity for a time out. One time a daughter, who refused to stay seated at a wedding reception, asked her father if he would allow her to count it as two and a half fingers instead of three!

Aaron 24, says:

My dad was a very quiet, strong leader who seldom raised his voice. However, his eyebrows said volumes to my brothers and I. If we were horsing around in the house and getting rowdy, he would lower his newspaper and raise one eyebrow. Somehow we all knew that meant "take it outside and slow down." As young men when we wanted permission to borrow the car, or take a school trip, or jump in the river, when his eyebrow moved up, we knew we had to have some good reasons for asking or a solution to share. It was almost as if his eyebrow was saying "So, how are you going to solve this?" It is funny because we all grew up to be good problem-solvers and certainly much better at reading body language than our peers."

Some of the strongest messages are sent without words. A hug, wink, smile, pat on the back or just a wink can speak volumes. It indicates to the child that you care and are seeing him as an individual.

Use encouragement instead of criticism

A very effective way of communicating is to write notes or letters. These give you an opportunity to do an Encouragement Sandwich:

1. Start off with a slice of the bread of life. For example, "I really admire the way you are learning to take better care of your things."
2. Next, add a little mayo spread lightly, "I felt happy when I saw you hang up your new jacket last night."
3. Then, the slice of sharp cheese, "However, I noticed you left your bike outside in the rain again."
4. On top of the cheese, a little spicy mustard to catch their attention, "Please put it away every night or we will have to lock it up for a week each time it is left out.".

5. Finally, another slice of bread, "All in all, you are a responsible kid and I have confidence you will choose to take better care of your bike."

Do they get the message of the mistake of leaving the bike out? Yes, but it is not by attacking them personally.

Encouragement is the process of focusing on your children's assets and strengths in order to build their self-confidence and feelings of worth. We need to convey through words and gestures that we appreciate their efforts and improvements, not just their accomplishments. We need to make sure they understand our love and acceptance is not dependent on their behavior or winning the prize in soccer.

Say Yes instead of No

Jack Canfield of *Chicken Soup for the Soul* often cites a study done by some graduate students who followed a normal group of two-year olds around for a day. These average kids from average homes received 432 negative statements as opposed to 32 positive statements daily. The teachers, aides and other children were constantly saying, "Don't touch that." "No, it is done this way." "No, you are not big enough."

The national PTO (Parent Teacher Organization) found the ratio of praise to criticism of school age children to be 18 negative to each positive. It is such automatic action to state things in the negative. We have to learn the words to use to encourage our children.

Some children are convinced their parents only know the word NO. For them saying no, not and don't are mindless and reflex answers to many harmless and interesting requests their children make.

Michael Lazier, who wrote the book "The Attraction Factor" says,

> "It is no wonder that toddlers and children tune us out when we tell them no. They have heard it so much, that it loses its impact. How about re-phrasing some of your answers in a more positive way?
> "Yes, you may have a cookie when you have finished your dinner." "Yes I know you want to wear shorts today, but shorts are for summer days."

Guidelines for What You Can Do

When a child is growing and learning it is imperative that guidelines are set and enforced. But you will find much less rebellion if you emphasize what they *can do*, rather than what they can't do, and then follow through with consequences when they decide to break the rules.

Saying yes is a way to honor and respect the child and give them experience in having power enough to make some of their own decisions.

Teens especially need lots of yeses in their lives. They are ready to expand their world and are looking for more responsibility.

One time my husband Dwain told our daughter, who had been bugging to drive with only her learner's permit, "Yes, you may take the car and all your friends to the mall, but Grandma has to go with you." She stopped asking to use the car, at least for a little while.

Many people are so used to looking at life in a pessimistic way that they don't realize how many negative words, phrases and messages they are sending out.

Tell Them What You Do Want

Add some information here

Please remember there is a big difference between phrasing answers to requests in a positive voice and indiscriminately allowing the child to run the show.

You are the adult and they look to you for guidance and boundaries. If you can't think of a way to phrase an answer positively, say "hmm, sounds interesting. Can I think about it for a bit?" Or even, "I can see why you would want to do that; bring me some more information." This leaves the door open to cooperation and conversation instead of anger.

Amanda 9 years old:

"The thing I hate the most is when grown ups won't listen. They say things like 'oh, you are so smart" and then when you try to tell them about a better way to do something, they get mad. I think they don't really want kids, they want robots!

Spanking and screaming are not affective teachers.

No discussion on discipline would be complete without commenting on spanking. Did we do it to our children? Yes, very, very rarely and only to emphasize strongly a lesson.

We did not do more than one smack on a covered bottom and called it an exclamation point. Do our children remember it? Yes, the few who had to be given an exclamation point to help them remember also remember what we were trying to teach.

Do you know what lessons they don't remember? The hundreds of times we ended up yelling out of frustration. As adults they tell us now, that a smack on the bottom or on the hand would have been easier than the two-hour lecture.

When You Scream, You Can't Hear

Unfortunately, there is a whole generation of young parents who grew up with abusive punishment that have promised themselves they will never spank. The problem is the same anger and frustration that fueled the old methods of corporal punishment, now fuels shouting hurtful things, which harm the child deeply.

When you are yelling, you can't listen and when you can't listen, you can't teach. And remember to discipline is to teach, not punish.

The best way to remind you is to STOP and think, "Would I yell this loud at a co-worker? A parent? A neighbor? A clerk in the store? Then why do I feel okay yelling at or smacking my child? It is so much more effective to admit, "I'm so angry that your clothes aren't on and we have to leave in three minutes, that it is best if I leave before I say something I will be sorry for. The carpool is leaving soon and you will either be dressed or go in your pajamas, you choose." And then go to the car and cool down a bit.

No matter how you disguise it, spanking and yelling abusive words is an excuse for a large adult to overpower a small child. Because they are both done in anger, it creates a potentially explosive situation.

Many of the frustrations between parent and child come from the fact that, while we love the child, we would appreciate them more if they were who we wanted them to be.

By respecting each child's interests, abilities, strengths and personalities, parents foster self-esteem and instill value in the individual that can have potential for long lasting harm. There are better ways to get cooperation in the family.

David age 10

If I could give some advice to parents it would be: if your kid does something wrong, don't say bad words and swear at him. Just say something like "Try not to do that again, please clean it up." I don't think adults know how much that hurts when they swear at kids. It makes them feel so bad. Sometimes she will say things like G**D++it, I ****ing hate it when you do that. And if you are going to say something good, really mean it. Don't just ignore the kid and then say something like "Good job, now run on, I'm busy." They should only say things that make a kid feel good. Once my mom said, "Go away, I hate you." That really hurt my feelings. Even though she apologized later, it still really hurt.

I have taught myself to think "Hey everyone makes mistakes. It was just one mistake. It's not the end of the world." Sometimes I go outside and pet the dogs or go for a walk and either in my mind or out loud say, "Don't feel so bad about something so little, just get on with your life. You are okay."

Eliminate "who's at fault."

If we can shift the emphasis in life and in the family from being right to being effective, it will make for a stronger, more cohesive unit. Accidents happen. Those children who have either been blamed or shifted the blame to someone else have a hard time with self-identity. They don't feel confident stepping out of their comfort zone, for fear they will make a mistake and be called on it.

Just the phrasing can make such a difference:

"Who left the gate open so the dog got out?" to, ""Hey, everybody, the gate was accidentally left open, let's go find the dog."

Or:

"Why are you two fighting again? Why can't you get along? Who started it this time?" to, "I can't think with the noise, you kids have two choices: go play outside together nicely or go to your rooms until you can treat each other with respect."

Dr. Wayne Dyer in his wonderful book "What Do You Really Want for Your Children" says, "Eliminate the "who's at fault" syndrome in your home, and insert a "let's find a solution" pattern. Finding out who is to blame and assigning blame are senseless activities that only teach children to become blamers. Instead of looking for problems, look for solutions. Blame solves nothing, but solutions are there if you can get past the notion of finding fault."

Instead of having family fights about who did what to whom, teach your children to think in more creative, solution oriented ways. By doing this, you will be teaching them a far more valuable lesson about being responsible for their own feelings and reactions in life.

Be aware of your facial expressions.

Verbal language is the communication of instruction and may only be absorbed 10-20% of the time. But body language is the communication of relationships and is understood and retained 70-90% of the time. Latest studies on the brain development also indicate that children and teenagers have trouble reading facial expressions and tend to clump them into general categories like angry, sad, happy and scared, as opposed to various gradients or degrees of each.

Judy, old enough to know better
"One time our son said, 'Quit yelling at me.'
When I replied that I wasn't yelling, but simply making a request in a normal voice, once again he taught me a lesson as only children can do 'Well, your voice may not be yelling, but your face was.' I realized that my mind was on a problem at work

and my face conveyed the message of anger. He 'saw' the angry expression much more vividly than he 'heard' the request."

Just as some children are dyslexic (have problems understanding and interpreting words), many children are dyssemic (difficulty in using and understanding nonverbal signs and signals).

You may have heard it described as a non-verbal learning disability. This is a major impediment to making friends and sustaining relationships. Nowicki and Duke in their book **"Helping the Child who doesn't Fit In"** found that about 10% of children are dyssemic to some degree.

It is important if your child just doesn't "get it" when you are starting to lose patience or they have crossed the line of appropriate behavior, that you consider he or she may be unable to read and interpret non-verbal body language.

There are ways to correct and teach skills that will assist them and you to read and interpret non-verbal language.

It is possible to alter the course of your child's life by teaching life skills to overcome this disability. It will take time and effort on your part, but it will make communication easier in your home and in his life.

If your child has difficulty making and keeping friends, you will want to check out **The Left Out Child—The Importance of Friendship** at http://bit.ly/LeftOutChild or for really in-depth study, please check out the excellent non-verbal learning disorder website www.nldline.com.

Treat each child as an individual.

"It's not fair" or even "you love him/her the best!" has been the battle cry of families across the world forever. Even Cain and Able had sibling rivalry going on. It isn't easy or even possible to treat all children the same. They aren't the same. They are unique and special individuals and each has special and unique gifts to bring to the world.

Our job as adults is to help the child identify those special gifts and to learn to value and enhance them. This is sometimes hard in a large family or if one child is especially gifted or even handicapped.

If your parenting method worked for one child but is not working for the next child, then change your methods with the second child. Although many aspects of parenting will be the same, each child is different with different needs and experiences. Instead of comparing children or setting them up to compete with one another for your affection and approval, celebrate their differences.

Many parents, who have set such high expectations for themselves, tend to see imperfections or mistakes by their children as signs they have somehow failed. They keep trying to create this "ideal child." If we try to force a child to fit into a mold or to be "like their older brother," we risk sending them a message that we don't love them for who they are, but only for how close they can come to our ideal.

Adele Faber and Elaine Mazlish in their great book "Siblings without Rivalry," gave the following suggestion:

> *"Here is what helped me break the pattern. Whenever I was tempted to compare one child to another, I would say to myself, STOP! DON'T! Whatever you want to tell this child can be said directly, without any reference to his brother. The key word is 'describe.' Describe what you see. Or describe what you like. Or describe what you don't like. Or describe what needs to be done. The important thing is to stick with the issue of this one child's behavior. Nothing his brother is or isn't doing has anything to do with him."*

Many of the frustrations between parent and child come from the fact that while we love the child, we would appreciate them more if they were who we wanted them to be. By respecting each child's interests, abilities, strengths and personalities, parents foster self-esteem and instill value in the individual.

Lettie, age 7

"My dad says I have 'Bambie eyes' when I want something. If I know that if I am in trouble, I can look at him and smile and he will usually say something like, 'Okay, but don't do it again.' My brother, who is 11, says it isn't fair, because he doesn't get away with stuff. I don't think it is fair either, but I still do it.

Be careful of using abusive adjectives—they really hurt.

If you and your child were in a museum and you said, "Wow, look at that ugly painting. It stinks! The colors are wrong. It is a dud! How could anyone in their right mind pay good money for that?" The people around you might laugh in agreement or frown in embarrassment or maybe even be offended and leave, but the painting wouldn't care.

It wouldn't be embarrassed, or hurt or insulted. It would never change because of what you thought and said about it. The painting would not cringe and ache inside from the criticism. It would just hang there on the wall until it was moved.

But when you call your living, breathing child ugly or worthless, it does hurt deeply. Something happens to the child on a cellular level. Not only are there physical reactions but it hurts his soul. When a child is told repeatedly that he is stupid or ugly or any other derogatory adjective, he believes you. He may argue or deny it the first few times, but eventually he too will buy into the label. All too soon, it will become a self-fulfilling prophecy. He will act ugly and stupid by misbehaving or he will give up and be reconciled to failure.

Be very careful in the use of nicknames or labels. Even if you think it is harmless to call your daughter klutz or even Princess, it is sending a message to the child to live up to the title. These daily reminders are actually repetitive reinforces of how you see them and they become embedded in their sub-conscious.

Shelby age 12
One time my dad said he was going to start calling me Adolph Hitler because I was being bossy and he said I was acting like a little dictator. My brother picked it up and now he calls me that all the time and he told his friends. I get really embarrassed and hate it and him when he teases me like that.

Recognize effort and improvement:

Many times what Mary can't do in January; she will be able to handle in June. A lot of mastery of tasks depends on physical, social and psychological levels of development.

As veteran parents and teachers can attest, the road to independence is filled with potholes and temporary detours, and children can't follow maps. It is so easy when they are babies and toddlers and the progress is always a reward and forward moving. We are so tickled every time they reach a milestone of rolling over, sitting up, saying their first word etc. But as children get older, we tend to expect more from them on a consistent basis.

As parents, we need to be sensitive to signs of improvement. Do not insist on perfection right off or ever, but do reinforce when they are getting better. Immediate reinforcement is most effective. Try complimenting the child for completing short tasks and then gradually lengthen the tasks.

If you can't reinforce right away, take time later to remind him of how much he has improved in that area and that you have confidence he will soon be able to do the whole job. I remember a phrase that I repeated over and over, as I was potty training a child who was much less interested than I in the process. It was, "To get a good habit going, reward every time. To keep it going, reward intermittently."

)(This whole section may be moved somewhere else, It just takes up room here. Or then again, it may further explain what I am trying to teach)

They may physically be able to sort the dirty clothes, but be distracted by friends, TV or daydreams. So when they make the effort to do the job, but fall short of completion, we have a couple of options: 1) get mad, do it ourselves, berate the child and throw it in their face for the next twenty years or 2) say, (I statement-see number___) "When I saw the clothes had not been finished being sorted as you had agreed, I was annoyed because that meant the washing could not be done for the family. A big part of finishing a job is getting started, and you did that. But the most important part of the job is finishing, so you have two choices: 1) I will do the sorting and finish the job and you will forgo TV for the week or 2) you will finish the job as agreed and work on remembering to finish tasks. To feel confident, children and adults must feel useful and know their contributions count in helping life work smoothly for the family. It may be that the child above is not ready to sort the clothes, but can contribute by bringing the dirty clothes to the laundry room. If you try again in a few weeks or months, the child may be ready to complete the job. Also, make sure you are sincere in comments on how the child's efforts help the family and are appreciated.

Don't punish them for telling the truth.

If they know they will get an angry response for admitting to spilling the milk or eating the last cookie, of course they will try to shift the blame. When they tell you the truth, praise them for being honest and then tell them you can always work out any problem together.

I have found that confronting my kids about something they obviously did almost forced them into a lie.

It was better if I just stated the facts by saying, "I see money is missing from the top of the dresser. Let's talk about how you are going to repay it and what happens when you take something without permission."

Kids are always testing parents by lying, fibbing or blaming imaginary friends. We need to make it clear that telling the truth is a value we have in our family and fibbing won't be tolerated. Believe it or not, children feel more secure knowing what the boundaries are and they won't be punished for telling the truth.

As an aside to this, I need to ask you to examine how you model integrity and truth telling. Have you ever told your children to tell someone on the phone that you weren't home?

Have they ever heard you fib about buying something in order to keep your spouse from finding out how much you spent?

These actions send mixed messages to children. Rightfully, they may think lying is acceptable if you can get away with it. We all need to model the behavior we expect from our children.

If your child has a serious problem lying or blaming others, see the book *"It's Not My Fault; Helping Your Children to be Non-blamers and to tell the truth (Most of the time),"* at www.artichokepress.com.

Zig Ziglar, Great Grandfather and International Motivational speaker and author, says:

> *"Your children pay more attention to what you do than what you say. If you set the example, you won't need to make many rules. Rules without a relationship lead to rebellion. A few rules and a good example can lay the basis for a marvelous relationship and raising of positive, morally sound, successful youngsters."*

Be both firm and kind in discipline.

Firmness refers to your follow-through behavior when you are correcting a child. Kindness refers to the manner in which you present the situation and the consequence. By stating your requests in an assertive, calm voice, you will model effective communication skills for the family.

For consequences to be effective, the children must see them as logical. For instance: "You know the rule about not riding your bike in the street. Since you made the choice to do it anyway, you will have to put the bike in the garage for the rest of the week. Do you want me to help you put it away or can you do it yourself?"

Don't allow the child to argue about the consequence for her choice. If you give in after your child has a tantrum, then he will learn to repeat the behavior on the chance that you may give in again.

Simply restate the position and if she starts to argue, then you can say "I see you have chosen to put it away yourself, when you come in the house maybe you can put a puzzle together."

Avoid fighting, or yelling which shows a lack of respect for the other person. Giving in indicates a lack of respect for yourself.

Praise in public, correct in private

No one likes to feel they are on trial, especially in front of their friends or siblings. A humiliating or embarrassing moment can stick with a person for the rest of their life, long after the incident that caused it has been forgotten.

As adults, we need to treat the child and the mistake with respect. We need to use a mistake as a teaching moment rather than judgment day. Here is a good mantra to recite to yourself when you are tempted to correct your son at the soccer game: **"praise in public, correct in private."**

Devin, age 14
My dad got thrown out of a basketball game at the YMCA one time because he was swearing at the referee. He gets so riled up and yells at me from the stands to 'grab the ball' and I can't just grab the ball. I don't even like basketball when he is going to be there. I just want to play for fun not the NBA

Distinguish between minor mishaps and major problems.

A minor mishap can be a wonderful teaching tool in helping your child cope with disappointment, but gain an understanding that some things are unpleasant or annoying, but are not necessarily tragic or catastrophic. To do this, you may have to recognize that the jerk in front of you during rush hour that doesn't use his turn signal is not worth getting so upset over. By modeling appropriate anger you are teaching a valuable lesson in self-control.

Suppose your child loses a jacket (something everybody does come spring and fall). How do you react? The temptation, especially if you are reverting to old habits, is to start by blaming. "How could you have been so careless? Don't you realize what jackets cost? When are you going to learn to take better care of your possessions? Do you know how hard I had to work to earn the money to buy that jacket?" yadayadayadyadya**.**

There are a thousand different accusations we can fling at the child to convince him that we care more about the $12 jacket than we do about him.

Why not try something sympathy, "Oh wow, that was your favorite one wasn't it?" Or maybe something to show you are on his side, even when bad things happens in life. "When I lose things, it helps me to close my eyes and try to retrace my steps. Sometimes it just pops into my head where I left it." Or even, "Come on, let's go back to the soccer field and see if you might have left it there."

He knows there are consequences, both natural and logical so he will either have to pay for a new jacket or wear an old one, but **at least he will do so with his spirit intact.**

My mother used to say, "Don't waste the same energy over a broken egg that you would over a broken leg."

Model Forgiveness

Many people feel as though it is a sign of weakness to apologize for doing something that hurt someone else's feelings. On the contrary, it shows that you are a compassionate, kind person who regrets hurting someone else and you want to resolve the matter and move on with life. Dr. Robert Schuller in his book *"The Be (Happy) Attitudes,"* says that the two miracle working statements are; "I need help" and "I am sorry."

If we have offended our child with an impatient remark or unfair discipline, we need to model for them the 4 R's of correcting a mistake

1. Recognize (I realize that I was rude to you when your friend was here)
2. Remorse (I feel badly that I over reacted and yelled at you)
3. Restitution (I will apologize to your friend when he comes again.)
4. Resolve (You have my promise that I will try not to embarrass you in front of your friends.)

True forgiveness occurs on a cellular level. I would like to recommend the book of a friend and colleague; Dr. Ira Byock called "The Four Things that matter Most." Even though Dr. Byock is an international leader in palliative (end-of-life) care, he is able to teach us the transformation of speaking the unspoken in daily life. He has found the four phrases, please forgive me, I forgive you, thank you and I love you, carry enormous power. These four things that matter most can guide us through the tough times in our family relations and lead us to a conscious way of living that is filled with integrity and grace.

Be curious not furious. Ask questions.

One of the most important life skills you can teach your child is to be a problem solver. If we always tell them what to do, feel and be, they will be forever looking to others for validation and instruction. At a time when tempers are not flaring, for instance in a family council or after dinner and before reading aloud, ask your child "if you could change one thing about today, what would it be?" What made you happy, or sad, or discouraged, or full of confidence?" Then turn the tables and have them ask you the same questions.

This natural sharing leads to a communication and exchange of feelings that will stand you in good stead for the rest of your lives. It lets the child know you are truly interested in their feelings and observations. It also indicates to the child that you are willing to listen and learn from him.

Instead of telling them the solution or answer to a problem, ask, "What do you think would be fair?" Other good questions are, "How shall we solve this? Can you come up with three different solutions? What would happen if? How did you come to that conclusion? What makes you think that? Will you explain that to me? Can you give me some more information? Can tell me what you mean? How would you have handled that if it had happened to you?

The Families First motto is "**Be curious, not furious**" and it is a wonderful reminder to us to find out what our children are thinking, feeling and perceiving before we rush to judgment. It is so important that we develop our own motto or mantra of "let me understand. Let me show him/her that I understand by asking questions that do not automatically criticize or condemn."

In order to truly understand and discipline in a positive way, we need to listen to what our children are saying, both verbally and non-verbally. It is so easy for us to jump to conclusions, offer advice, give lectures, or hand out discipline without really listening to the story and how they might feel about the situation.

The most effective bonding moments come from truly listening to one another. How long has it been since you have simply listened to what your child was telling you? By giving our full attention when our child is talking, we show respect to them as individuals

(blah blah,,,,I need to redo this part.)

A final note to parents

So, dear friend, hopefully you have learned some ideas and techniques for making the home life a little more harmonious, and discipline a lot more effective.

If you don't get anything else out of this book, please remember the word discipline means to teach and lead. You are a teacher in every sense of the word.

The most important work you will ever do is the work you do to build and enhance relationships with those you love.

One hundred years from now, it will not matter what kind of car you drove, what you did for a living, how many hours you stayed at the office, how clean your house was or how many "things" you had acquired. What will matter is that you affected eternity and changed the world because you took the time and effort to be important in the life of your child.

For further reading on this and other parenting topics:

Books:

- Brazelton, T.B. 2001 *Touchpoints: Your Child's Emotional and Behavioral Development.* Cambridge, MA Perseus Publishing.
- Covey, S.R. 1997 *The Seven Habits of Highly Effective Families.* New York, Golden Books
- Faber, A. and E. Mazlish. 2002. *How to Talk so Kids Will Listen and Listen So Kids Will Talk.* New York: Quill/Harper Collins

- McGraw Dr. Phil. 2004. *Family First.* New York: Free Press.
- Cline, Foster and Fay, Jim *Parenting with Love and Logic*
- Ginott, Haim G., Goddard, Wallace and Ginott, Alice. *Between Parent and Child*

Websites:

- Positivedisciple.com
- The American Academy of Pediatrics
- www.arp.org
- Parenthood.com (helping families grow)
- posdis.org check under speaker

About The Author

Who is Judy H. Wright *aka Auntie Artichoke?*

& What's with the Artichoke?

Judy is a parent educator, family coach, and personal historian who has written more than 20 books, hundreds of articles and speaks internationally on family issues, including care giving. Trained as a ready to learn consultant, she works with Head Start organizations and child care resource centers. She also volunteers time writing end-of-life stories for Hospice.

She and Dwain, her husband of 40 years, have six grown children and seven grandchildren. They consider their greatest success in life that their children like themselves and each other. The honorary title of "Auntie" is given in many cultures to the wise women who guide and mentor others in life.

The artichoke also became a teaching lesson when Judy, with her young family, moved into military housing in California to find Artichokes in their yard. Given that it takes two years for the vegetable to flower, the original gardener never got to see the seeds of her labor. Many times, our actions and reactions in life are felt by people we will never meet, but we plant the seeds of kindness anyway.

The symbol of the artichoke has great meaning in her teaching and writing. As she works with families, she sees frequently only the outer edges are exposed and can be prickly, hard to open and sometimes bitter to the taste. They are closed to new ideas or methods. Many families prefer the known over the unknown, even when the old patterns and skills are not serving them well.

But as you expose the artichoke and people to warmth, caring, and time, gradually the leaves begin to open and expose the real treasure—the heart.

You will enjoy Judy's approachable manner, wonderful storytelling and common-sense solutions gleaned from working with hundreds of families and organizations just like yours. Your encounter with Judy will leave you feeling inspired, entertained and especially motivated. Visit Judy's website for excellent references and a full listing of books, workshop topics, tele-classes and testimonials.

To make arrangements for your group or organization to enjoy having Judy present a keynote address, workshop or training session, please contact her at:

Judy H. Wright aka Auntie Artichoke,
the Storytelling Trainer

(406) 549-9813,
Email: Judy@ArtichokePress.com

www.ArtichokePress.com

"Finding the heart of the story in the journey of life."

Free eBook at www.UseEncouragingWords.com

"Visiting with Judy is like having a cup of tea with a loving auntie."

"We are all grateful for the incredible work you do to birth these stories."

Resources for Parents, Teachers and other Caring Adults

http://www.ArticlesbyJudy.com Free articles on relationships/parenting/grief/personal development Free to use in your blog-just keep content and contact info intact.

http://www.JudyHWright.com Personal website for Judy H. Wright, including blog and articles. Connect with Judy for empowerment coaching and inspirational speaking engagements.

http://www.ArtichokePress.com Main website for Judy H Wright, full listing of books, workshops, radio shows, tele-classes. Free report available.

http://www.BounceBackPerson.com Site for Judy's latest book, *Out Of Balance? Be a Bounce Back Person*. Includes bonus items.

http://www.EmpowermentWithJudy.com Mentoring and MasterMind. Not empowerment for Judy or by Judy, but with Judy. Walking life's journey together.

http://www.KidsChoresandMore.com Site for Judy's book, *Kids, Chores, And More*. Includes bonus items. Free report available.

http://www.TheLeftOutChild.com Site for the importance of friendship, Sign up for our free e-course

http://www.AskAuntieArtichoke.com   Blog for parenting and relationships. Please leave comments and questions. You will be glad you did.

http://www.IfDeathIsNear.com   Blog for those facing the loss of a loved one.

http://www.DeathOfMyPet.com   Book and bonus items for someone who has lost a beloved pet.. Excellent stories and resources for pet lovers.

http://www.CyberbullyingHelp.com   Main site for bullying and cyberbullying assistance. Free report and connections to other blogs and websites. Leave comments and share your story.

http://www.UseEncouragingWords.com   Main site for free e-book on the power of words and communication.

http://www.DisciplineYesPunishNo.com   Site for alternatives to punishment. Transform and strengthen your family connections and communications.

http://www.WelcomeAbundance.com   Methods of earning passive streams of income.

http://www.EncourageSelfConfidence.com   Site for Judy's book, **Using Encouraging Words to Motivate Positive Action** and bonus items about building self-confidence with encouraging words.

http://www.4lifehappykids.com/judy   Goal setting and teaching your children the Law of Attraction.

http://www.judyhwright.com/gigglebaby   Giggle Baby – Find great clothes and creative products for your children

Thank you for joining our community of kind, thoughtful people who want to model and teach kindness, tolerance and respect for all.

Printed in Great Britain
by Amazon